God's
Creative
Power®
for Healing

by
Charles Capps

Unless otherwise indicated, all Scripture quotations are taken from the *King James Version* of the Bible.

Scripture quotations marked AMP are taken from *The Amplified Bible, Old Testament* copyright © 1965, 1987 by Zondervan Corporation. *New Testament* copyright © 1958, 1987 by the Lockman Foundation. Used by Permission.

GOD'S CREATIVE POWER® FOR HEALING

11 10 09   70 69 68

Over 1 million in print

God's Creative Power® for Healing
ISBN: 978-0-9820320-0-8
Formerly ISBN: 978-0-89274-815-0

Copyright © 1991 by Charles Capps
P.O. Box 69
England, Arkansas 72046

Published by Capps Publishing
P.O. Box 69
England, AR 72046

CONTENTS

Introduction

Medical science tells us there are many incurable diseases such as some forms of cancer, arthritis, heart disease and AIDS, just to name a few. This book presents a supernatural help to all people with incurable diseases. God's Word is supernatural. Mixing faith with God's Word by speaking it out of your mouth is a means of applying God's medicine. The rest is up to the individual as to whether or not they have the confidence to take God's medicine on a regular basis.

The purpose of this book is to reveal principles from God's Word and instruct you in how to cooperate with and apply these principles to obtain healing. Many today are seeking healing but yet they talk sickness and suffering until they establish that image in them. Their thoughts and words produce a vivid blueprint and they live within the bounds and limitations of that blueprint. In the following chapters you will learn how to make that blueprint line up with the Word of God.

1
Building Blocks
of Life or Death

Your words are building blocks of which you construct your life and future. Your words set the cornerstones of your life, and you live within the confines of that boundary you create with your own words. Situations, circumstances and conditions are all subject to change, but with the support of your words you can establish them in your life forever.

The following article, entitled "Patient Knows Best," appeared in the August 1991 issue of *The Reader's Digest:*

"A person's answer to the question, 'Is your health excellent, good, fair or poor?' is a remarkable predictor of who will live or die over the next four years according to new findings.

A study of more than 2800 men and women 65 and older found that those who

who rate their health 'poor' are four to five
times more likely to die in the next four years
than those who rate their health 'excellent.'
This was the case even if examinations show
the respondents to be in comparable health.

These findings are supported by a review
of five other large studies, totaling 23,000
people, which reached similar conclusions,
according to Ellen Idler, a sociologist at
Rutgers University, and epidemiologist
Stanislav Kasl of Yale University School of
Medicine, co-authors of the new study.''

People that have an image of themselves being in poor health will talk about poor health. Even though they may be in good health, they seem to live out the reality of the image they have of themselves even unto death.

This would confirm Proverbs 18:21, **Death and life are in the power of the tongue: and they that love it shall eat the fruit thereof.**

What you believe and speak not only

affects your body *but your immune system as well*. Your words become either a blessing or a curse to you.

Jesus put it this way: **A good man out of the good treasure of his heart bringeth forth that which is good; and an evil man out of the evil treasure of his heart bringeth forth that which is evil: for of the abundance of the heart his mouth speaketh** (Luke 6:45).

I am convinced from my study of the Word of God that your own words can change your immune system for better or worse. (James 3:2-7.) The words you speak are vital to your health and well being. I believe there are some diseases that will never be cured unless people learn to speak the language of health that the body understands. God's Word is infused (engrafted) into you by giving voice to His Word with your own mouth, and this is the language of health to your body.

A continual affirmation of God's Word in faith will build into your immune system a supernatural anointing that is capable of eliminating sickness and disease in a natural manner.

God's Building Blocks

Here are a few of many scriptural reasons why I believe this so strongly:

Thou shalt also decree a thing, and it shall be established unto thee: and the light shall shine upon thy ways.

Job 22:28

A fool's mouth is his destruction, and his lips are the snare of his soul.

Proverbs 18:7

For verily I say unto you, That whosoever shall say unto this mountain, Be thou removed, and be thou cast into the sea; and shall not doubt in his heart, but shall believe that those things which he saith shall come to pass; he shall have whatsoever he saith.

Mark 11:23

A man's heart deviseth his way: but the Lord directeth his steps.

Proverbs 16:9

A man's belly shall be satisfied with the fruit of his mouth; and with the increase of his lips shall he be filled. Death and life are in the power of the tongue: and they that love it shall eat the fruit thereof.

Proverbs 18:20,21

...the tongue is a fire, a world of iniquity: so is the tongue among our members, that it defileth the whole body, and setteth on fire the course of nature; and it is set on fire of hell.

James 3:6

Whoso keepeth his mouth and his tongue keepeth his soul from troubles.

Proverbs 21:23

I create the fruit of the lips; Peace, peace to him that is far off, and to him that is near, saith the Lord; and I will heal him.

Isaiah 57:19

The mouth of a righteous man is a well of life.

Proverbs 10:11

...the mouth of the upright shall deliver them.

Proverbs 12:6

A man shall be satisfied with good by the fruit of his mouth.

Proverbs 12:14

...the tongue of the wise is health.

Proverbs 12:18

He that keepeth his mouth keepeth his life.

Proverbs 13:3

...the lips of the wise shall preserve them.

Proverbs 14:3

A wholesome tongue is a tree of life: but perverseness therein is a breach in the spirit.

Proverbs 15:4

A gentle tongue [with its healing power] is a tree of life, but willful contrariness in it breaks down the spirit.

Proverbs 15:4 AMP

The tongue of the wise useth knowledge aright.

Proverbs 15:2

The heart of the wise teacheth his mouth, and addeth learning to his lips.

Proverbs 16:23

Pleasant words are as an honeycomb, sweet to the soul, and health to the bones.

Proverbs 16:24

You can see from these few references that God's Word has a lot to say about words and their effects on you and your health.

2
Divine Healing
Is a Spiritual Cure

Medical science aids healing through physical means by administering medicine into the physical body. God's Divine Healing is Spiritual. It is administered through the human spirit. (1 Cor. 2:9-12.) Psalm 107:20 tells us that God sent His Word and healed THEM. Notice that it didn't say that God sent his Word *to heal* but He sent His Word *and HEALED*. God considers it done. God is no respecter of persons, but He does respect FAITH in His Word.

> **My son, attend to my words; incline thine ear unto my sayings.**
>
> **Let them not depart from thine eyes; keep them in the midst of thine heart.**
>
> **For they are life unto those that find them, and health to all their flesh.**
>
> Proverbs 4:20-22

First of all notice that God's Word is LIFE. It is also HEALTH, or medicine to all your flesh. God's Word WILL HEAL YOUR BODY, but it does it through spiritual means. Healing can be received into the human spirit through the Word. Once it is conceived there, it permeates the physical body.

Just as you would take medicine into your physical body to aid healing by physical means, so YOU MUST RECEIVE God's WORD concerning healing into your spirit for supernatural healing.

The Engrafted Word

God's Word is PERFECT SPIRITUAL LAW. Ps. 19:7.) It is SUPERNATURAL MEDICINE. It works through the human spirit and is a spiritual cure, but like any other medicine, it must be applied on a regular basis. You MUST SPEAK GOD'S WORD to your individual circumstance or situation — someone else can't do it for you. James 1:21 admonishes us to **receive with meekness the engrafted word, which is able to save your souls.** Once the

13

Word of God is engrafted into your spirit, it produces results in the body as well.

Jesus said, **If ye abide in me, and my words abide in you, ye shall ask what ye will, and it shall be done unto you** (John 15:7). When God's Word becomes engrafted or infused into your spirit it has become a part of you. It cannot be separated from you! It is not only your thought and affirmation, IT IS YOU! THE WORD MADE FLESH. Then your flesh will reflect the life of that Word. When God's Word concerning healing takes root in your flesh, it becomes greater than disease and healing is the result.

The image that the Word creates in you is already a reality in the spirit realm. When you speak God's Word from your heart, then faith gives substance to the promises of God. Your faith frames your world daily. Jesus made it very plain — "a good man out of the good treasure of his heart brings forth good things..." (Matt. 12:35).

14

In the first Chapter of Genesis you will notice that every time God spoke, creation took place! Words are the CARRIERS OF FAITH! **The worlds were framed by the word of God** (Heb. 11:3). Without words, there wouldn't have been any creation. Your words create images and eventually you will live out the reality of that image.

Every time you speak your faith, it creates a stronger image inside you. If it is healing you desire, the healing image is created by God's Word and your continual affirmation and agreement with it. Eventually that image will be perfected by the Word of God and you will begin to see yourself well. When the Word is engrafted into you it infuses its life into you. (John 6:63; Rom. 8:11.)

Faith Possesses Reality

An example of this is found in Mark 5:25-28, where the woman with the issue of blood said, **If I may touch but his clothes, I shall be whole.** She continued to speak until she SAW HERSELF WELL!

15

This woman hoped to be healed as she pressed through the crowd. The *Amplified Bible* says: "For she kept saying, If I only touch His garments, I shall be restored to health."

That hope was her goal, but she didn't FEEL HEALED, she didn't LOOK HEALED. But she began filling hope with faith filled words, "I shall be restored to health. I SHALL BE restored to health. I shall be... I SHALL BE..."

I am sure her head said "WHEN?" "You don't LOOK ANY BETTER, you are NOT ANY BETTER!"

Then she began to answer human reasoning by being more specific — "When I touch His garment I shall be restored to health."

She was filling her HOPE with a FAITH IMAGE. She set her own point of contact to receive her healing. Her words penetrated her spirit and she began to see herself well. That "grow worse" image of despair and defeat had to give way to the FAITH FILLED WORDS that came from her own mouth.

When she touched His clothes, *her touch* of faith made a demand on the covenant of God and the ANOINTING that was upon Jesus.

What she was saying was her *faith talking*. When she acted out what she said and touched His garment, that faith that was in her BECAME THE SUBSTANCE of her hope, and her words became a living reality.

Faith Gives Substance to Hope

Notice it was her faith that made a demand on the healing anointing that was upon Jesus. Faith gave substance to her hope and healing was manifested IN HER BODY.

Faith is the substance of things hoped for (Heb. 11:1). Hope is important but hope lacks substance until filled with faith. HOPE is only a goal-setter. Her HOPE was to be healed, but hope DIDN'T HEAL HER! FAITH gave substance to her hope.

Her faith gave substance to and brought about the manifestation of healing that was already hers because of the covenant. But she

17

had to call for it. Look at the words of Jesus: "All things are possible to them that believe... (Mark 9:23) ...if you had faith as a seed you should say (Luke 17:6) ...he that believeth hath (John 3:36) ...whosoever shall say...he shall have..." (Mark 11:23,24.) It is the Bible principle of BELIEVING AND CALLING FOR THINGS THAT ARE NOT YET MANIFEST.

The words of Jesus ring very clear concerning this matter. **Daughter,** THY FAITH HATH MADE THEE WHOLE... (Mark 5:34). Giving voice to your faith in God's Word can also make you whole.

3

God's Word Is Medicine

God's Word is spoken of in Proverbs 4:22 as being medicine to all our flesh. It is the most powerful medicine available today, and it is capable of healing your body without side effects.

Psalm 107:20 tells us that God sent His Word and healed...According to Isaiah 53:5,6 and 1 Peter 2:24, healing is a fact as far as God is concerned. It belongs to us because healing was in the atonement. (Isa. 53:5,6.)

Our confession of the Word of God calls for healing which is already ours but is not in manifestation in our bodies.

No, I am not teaching against doctors or medicine. But don't depend on doctors or medicine alone to keep you healthy. There are some diseases that medical science cannot cure. But, if you need a doctor, see a doctor. Many lives are saved every year through medical help. There are medicines today that are beneficial in aiding the body's healing process.

If you are taking medicine, mix faith with it by saying, "I believe I receive my healing in Jesus' Name." Man's medicines will not heal you, and generally will not keep you from being healed. Yet there are some medicines today that have so many side effects they seem to be worse than the disease. So ask some questions and find out what you are taking. Most medicine will help hold down the symptoms while you are applying God's principles concerning healing and health.

I don't advocate that you throw your medicine away and rely on confession alone unless the Lord directs you to do so. It takes time to renew your mind and develop faith in your words as well as God's Word. But the things you are continually confessing eventually become a part of you. It is true, God has provided healing for us through His Word. But we must learn to appropriate that healing by making the Word a part of our daily vocabulary.

I believe by being taught properly and by practicing your faith you can grow to a point where it will be a common thing for you to receive healing through the Word of God. But it doesn't happen overnight. It takes time to develop your faith, so if you have a life or death situation where the doctors say if you don't have an operation immediately you will die — in other words, the disease has a head start on your faith — my advice would be to have the operation and believe God for a quick recovery. Use some common sense and don't do foolish things through spiritual pride and call it faith.

It takes time to develop faith to operate in these principles, so don't let anyone put you under condemnation for going to doctors or having an operation. In other words, operate on your level of faith, but don't stay on that level forever. Continue in God's Word until you develop faith in the healing power of God's Word.

God's Word is creative power. The worlds were framed by the Word of God. Confessing the Word of God can also change your world. It can change an image of sickness into an image of healing and health.

Operating in these principles is not easy. It takes discipline and commitment. It's not good enough to just read these confessions. I encourage you to confess the Word audibly over your body two or three times a day. Confess it with authority. It is not necessary for you to make these confessions before other people, for the words you speak are for your benefit.

Bad News and God's News

Doctors may have told you there is no hope for you medically, but you can always find supernatural HOPE from God's Word:

> ...they cry unto the Lord in their trouble, and he saveth them out of their distresses. He sent his word and healed them, and delivered them from their destructions.
>
> Psalm 107:19,20

So shall my word be that goeth forth out of my mouth: it shall not return unto me void, but it shall accomplish that which I please, and it shall prosper in the thing whereto I send it.

Isaiah 55:11

I create the fruit of the lips; Peace, peace to him that is far off, and to him that is near, saith the Lord; and I will heal him.

Isaiah 57:19

Returning God's Word to Him

God declares that His Word will not return to Him void. We are to return His Word by giving VOICE TO IT, and He will create the fruit of our lips. Confessing God's Word is a way you can fellowship with the Lord and increase your faith at the same time. I challenge you to affirm these scriptural confessions audibly three times a day. Don't let it become a hit and miss proposition. Make it a practice to take God's medicine on a regular basis, just as you would any other medicine. Then it will be LIFE to you and HEALTH to your flesh.

4

God's Medicine

To be spoken by mouth three times a day until faith comes, then once a day to maintain faith. If circumstances grow worse, double the dosage. There are no harmful side effects.*

Jesus is the Lord of my life. Sickness and disease have no power over me. I am forgiven and free from SIN AND GUILT. I am dead to sin and alive unto righteousness. (Col. 1:21,22.)

***

I am FREE from unforgiveness and strife. I forgive others as Christ has forgiven me, for the love of God is shed abroad in my heart by the Holy Ghost. (Matt. 6:12; Rom. 5:5.)

***

Jesus bore my sins in His Body on the tree; therefore I am dead to sin and alive unto God and by His stripes I am healed and made whole. (1 Pet. 2:24; Rom. 6:11; 2 Cor. 5:21.)

---

*These are not direct quotations from the Bible but these are paraphrased confessions based on the Scriptures under them.

24

***

Jesus bore my sickness and carried my pain. Therefore I give no place to sickness or pain. For God sent His Word and healed me. (Ps. 107:20.)

***

Father, because of Your Word I am an overcomer. I overcome the world, the flesh and the devil, by the Blood of the Lamb and the word of my testimony. (1 John 4:4, Rev. 12:11.)

***

You have given me abundant life. I receive that life through Your Word and it flows to every organ of my body bringing healing and health. (John 10:10; John 6:63.)

***

Heavenly Father, I attend to Your Word. I incline my ears to Your sayings. I will not let them depart from my eyes. I keep them in the midst of my heart, for they are life and healing to all my flesh. (Prov. 4:20-22.)

***

As God was with Moses, so is He with me. My eyes are not dim; neither are my natural forces abated. Blessed are my eyes for they see and my ears, for they hear. (Deut. 34:7.)

***

No evil will befall me, neither shall any plague come near my dwelling. For You have given your angels charge over me. They keep me in all my ways. In my pathway is life, healing and health. (Ps. 91:10,11; Prov. 12:28.)

***

Jesus took my infirmities and bore my sicknesses. Therefore I refuse to allow sickness to dominate my body. The Life of God flows within me bringing healing to every fiber of my being. (Matt. 8:17; John 6:63.)

I am redeemed from the curse. Galatians 3:13 is flowing in my blood stream. It flows to every cell of my body, restoring life and health. (Mark 11:23; Luke 17:6.)

***

The life of First Peter 2:24 is a reality in my flesh, restoring every cell of my body.

***

I present my body to God for it is the temple of the LIVING GOD. God dwells in me and HIS LIFE permeates my SPIRIT, SOUL and BODY so that I am filled with the fullness of God daily. (Rom. 12:1,2; John 14:20.)

***

My body is the temple of the HOLY GHOST. I make a demand on my body to release the right chemicals. My body is in perfect chemical balance. My pancreas secretes the proper amount of insulin for life and health. (1 Cor. 6:19.)

***

Heavenly Father, through Your Word You have imparted Your life to me. That life restores my body with every breath I breathe and every word I SPEAK. (John 6:63; Mark 11:23.)

***

That which God has not planted is dissolved and rooted out of my body in Jesus' name. First Peter 2:24 is engrafted into every fiber of my being and I am alive with the life of God. (Mark 11:23; John 6:63.)

27

Growths,
Tumors, and Arthritis

Jesus bore the curse for me; therefore, I forbid growths and tumors to inhabit my body. The life of God within me dissolves growths and tumors, and my strength and health is restored. (Matt. 16:19; John 14:13; Mark 11:23.)

***

Growths and tumors have no right to my body. They are a thing of the past for I am delivered from the authority of darkness. (Col. 1:13,14.)

***

Every organ and tissue of my body functions in the perfection that God created it to function. I forbid any malfunction in my body in Jesus' name. (Gen. 1:28,31.)

***

Father, Your Word has become a part of me. It is flowing in my bloodstream. It flows to every cell of my body, restoring and transforming my body. Your Word has become flesh; for You sent Your Word and healed me.   (James 1:21; Ps. 107:20; Prov. 13:3.)

***

Your Word is manifest in my body, causing growths to disappear.   Arthritis is a thing of the past.   I make a demand on my bones and joints to function properly in Jesus' Name. (Mark 11:23; Matt. 17:20.)

***

Heavenly Father, as I give voice to Your Word, the law of the Spirit of Life in Christ Jesus makes me free from the law of sin and death.   And your Life is energizing every cell of my body. (Rom. 8:12)

***

Arthritis, you must GO! Sicknesses MUST FLEE! Tumors can't exist in me, for the Spirit of God is upon me and the Word of God is within me.   Sickness, fear and oppression have no power over me for God's Word is my confession. (Mark 11:23.)

Heart and Blood

Thank You Father that I have a strong heart.   My heart beats with the rhythm of life. My blood flows to every cell of my body restoring life and health abundantly.   (Prov. 12:14; 14:30.)

My blood pressure is 120 over 80. The life of God flows in my blood and cleanses my arteries of all matter that does not pertain to life. (Mark 11:23.)

***

My heart beat is normal. My heart beats with the rhythm of life, carrying the life of God throughout my body restoring LIFE AND HEALTH ABUNDANTLY. (John 17:23; Eph. 2:22.)

***

I have a strong heart. Every heart beat floods my body with life and cleanses me of disease and pain. (Ex. 23:25; Mark 11:23.)

***

I command my blood cells to destroy every disease germ and virus that tries to inhabit my body. I command every cell of my body to be normal In Jesus' Name. (Rom. 5:17; Luke 17:6.)

***

Every cell that does not promote life and health in my body is cut off from its life source. My immune system will not allow tumorous growth to live in my body in Jesus' name. (Luke 17:6; Mark 11:23.)

***

I am redeemed from the curse of the law and my heart beats with the rhythm of life. The spirit and life of God's Word flows in me cleansing my blood of every disease and impurity. (Prov. 4:20-23.)

Arteries and Cells

In Jesus' Name, my arteries, will not shrink or become clogged. Arteries, you are clean, elastic and function as God created you to function. (Luke 17:6; Mark 11:23; Isa. 55:11; James 3:2-5.)

***

The law of the Spirit of Life in Christ Jesus has made me free from the law of sin and death; therefore, I will not allow sin, sickness or death to lord it over me. (Rom. 8:2; Rom. 6:13,14.)

***

The same Spirit that raised Jesus from the dead dwells in me, permeating His life

through my veins, sending healing throughout my body.   (Rom. 8:11.)

***

In Jesus' Name I forbid my body to be
deceived in any manner. Body, you will not
be deceived by any disease germ or virus.
Neither will you work against life or health in
any way. Every cell of my body supports life
and health. (Matt. 12:25; 35a.)

Immune System

My immune system grows stronger day by
day. I speak life to my immune system. I
forbid confusion in my immune system. The
same Spirit that raised Christ from the dead
dwells in me and quickens my immune system
with the life and wisdom of God, which
guards the life and health of my body.

Healthy Bones and Marrow

I speak to the *bones and joints* of my body.
I call you normal in Jesus' Name. My bones
and joints will not respond to any disease;
for the Spirit life of First Peter 2:24

permeates every bone and joint of my body with LIFE and HEALTH.

***

Father, I make a demand on my bones to produce perfect marrow. I make a demand on the marrow to produce pure blood that will ward off sickness and disease. My bones refuse any offense of the curse. (Prov. 16:24.)

***

I make a demand on my joints to function perfectly. There will be no pain or swelling in my joints. My joints refuse to allow anything that will hurt or destroy their normal function. (Prov. 17:22.)

Enforcing Life

Mix thoroughly with faith and authority. To be taken by word of mouth as often as needed to maintain health and life.

Body, I speak the Word of Faith to you. I demand that every organ perform a perfect work, for you are the temple of the HOLY GHOST; therefore, I charge you in the name of the Lord Jesus Christ and by the authority of His holy Word to be healed and made whole in Jesus' Name. (Prov. 12:18.)

***

Father, I resist the enemy in every form that he comes against me — I require my body to be strong and healthy, and I enforce it with Your Word. I reject the curse, and I enforce life in this body. (James 4:7.)

***

I will not die but live and declare the works of God. (Ps. 118:17)

***

You have forgiven all my iniquities; You have healed all my diseases; You have redeemed my life from destruction; You have satisfied my mouth with good things so that my youth is renewed as the eagles. (Ps. 103:2-5.)

***

Lord, You have blessed my food and water and have taken sickness away from me. Therefore I will fulfill the number of my days in health. (Ex. 23:25,26.)

5
Understanding the Principle

Now that you have gone through the scriptural confessions, let's look at the principle that could be the key to you being a partaker of God's provisions concerning your healing.

There is probably no other subject as important to your healing and health than the principle of CALLING THINGS THAT ARE NOT* We see in Romans 4:17-22 that Abraham became fully persuaded that God would do what He had promised. The way he became fully persuaded was by calling those things which were not manifest as though they were.

We pick up on this in verse seventeen:

(As it is written, I have made thee a father of many nations,) before him whom he believed, even God, who quickeneth the

---

*A complete teaching on this subject is available in the author's book, *Faith and Confession* (Tulsa: Harrison House, 1987).

dead, and calleth those things which be not as though they were.

Romans 4:17

Here Paul is referring to Genesis the 17th chapter. You will notice that God called Abram the father of nations before he had the promised child, and He taught Abram to do the same.

God changed Abram's name to Abraham, which meant "father of nations, or multitude." This was the means He used to convince Abraham to call for what he did not yet have in reality. God had established it by promise, but Abram had to call it into reality by mixing faith with God's Word.

Every time he said, "I am Abraham," he was calling things that were not yet manifest. Abraham did not deny that he was old. He didn't go around saying, "I'm not old," because he was old. But he said, "I am Abraham," (Father of Nations). This was God's method of helping him change his image, and it caused him to be fully persuaded.

Paul also gives us insight into this principle in 1 Corinthians 1:27,28:

> But God hath chosen the foolish things of the world to confound the wise; and God hath chosen the weak things of the world to confound the things which are mighty;

> And base things of the world, and things which are despised, hath God chosen, yea, and things which are not, to bring to nought things that are.

In other words God uses spiritual forces which are not seen to nullify natural things that are seen. This is the Bible principle of calling things that are not as though they were.

Then in 2 Corinthians 4:13, Paul says:

> We having the same spirit of faith, according as it is written, I believed, and therefore have I spoken; we also believe, and therefore speak.

Paul is quoting David when he said, **I believed, and therefore have I spoken....** In Psalm 118:17, David said, **I shall not die, but live, and declare the works of the Lord.**

When it comes to divine healing this is a vital principle. We should declare to ourselves what God's Word reveals about us, regardless of the circumstances or how we feel about it.

In Romans 10:6-8 Paul says that the righteousness which is of faith says ... the word is nigh thee, even in thy mouth and in thy heart.

Notice, the Word is *first in your mouth* and (then) in your heart. God's Word becomes engrafted into your heart as you speak it. There is nothing more important to your faith than declaring what God has said about you with your own voice. Giving voice to God's Word is a method of calling for things that God has given by promise and are not yet manifest.

When you do this, some would say that you are denying what exists, but that's not true at all. You are establishing what God has said to be true concerning healing even though it is not yet a reality in your body. You don't deny that sickness exists, *but you deny its right to exist in your body*, because you have been redeemed from the curse of the law and delivered from the authority of darkness. (Gal. 3:13; Col.1:13.)

God has also given you all things that pertain to life and godliness. These things belong to you. (2 Pet. 1:3,4.) When you are sick and confess that you are healed by the stripes of Jesus, *you are calling for what God has already given you, even though it is not yet manifest.*

This is God's method of calling things that are not as though they were until they are. There are some who have misunderstood this principle, and they call things that *are, as though they are not.* In other words, they deny what exists. But there is no power in denying that sickness exists. The power is in calling for healing and health by mixing faith with God's Word.

If you are sick, you don't deny that you are sick; yet, on the other hand, you don't want to always be confessing your sickness, for that will establish your present circumstance to you. Denying sickness won't make you well. But by mixing faith with God's Word, you are calling for the promise of God to be manifest in your body. This will cause you to be fully persuaded, and healing is the result.

There are some who would say you are lying if you confess you are healed when you are sick. No, you are simply calling for healing that God has already provided, even though it is not yet manifest in your body. What you are really doing is practicing God's medicine.

You are not trying to convince anyone that you are not sick, but you are simply proclaiming what God has said in His Word to be a fact, regardless of your present condition. The Word says, **by whose** (Jesus') **stripes ye** *were healed* (1 Pet. 2:24). Notice it is past tense as far as God is concerned, but not yet manifest in your body.

You are calling your body well according to Luke 17:5,6 and Mark 11:23. Your body is listening to you and it will obey you if you believe and doubt not in your heart. Your words have more effect on your body than anyone else's words.

Your body was created with the ability to heal itself, and if every part functions properly, it will. Some sickness is caused by a chemical imbalance in the body, and the part of the brain that controls the speech also controls the secretion of chemicals to the body. This sheds some more light on what Jesus said in Mark 11:23, **"...he shall have whatsoever he saith."**

Call What You Want

The one mistake that so many Christians make is that they call things that are, the way they are. By doing this they are establishing the present condition or circumstance in their heart, mind and also in their body.

I read an article many years ago about a lady that had a fever continually for several months. Doctors couldn't find anything wrong physically. They questioned her thoroughly and discovered that when she got upset about anything, she would always say, "that just burns me up." She used that phrase several times a day. They were not sure if it had anything to do with her condition or not, but they asked her not to use that phrase anymore. Within weeks, her body temperature was normal.

How many times have you said, "Every time I eat that, it makes me sick," "My back is just killing me," "Those kids make me so nervous" or, "I'm trying to take the flu"? Your own words are giving instruction to your body and your immune system will eventually respond to your instructions.

But God's method is to call for positive things, even though they are not yet a reality in your body. You call them *until they are manifest.* You have a God-given right to exercise authority over your body. In Romans 8:13, Paul tells us "∴. if you live after the flesh you shall die: but if you through the Spirit do mortify the deeds of the body, you shall live." Your flesh wants to say it the way it is, but your spirit, if trained properly, wants to say it the way God said it in His Word.

Your body will respond to the demands of the human spirit.

If you feed the spirit man God's Word, it will make demands on the flesh to line up with the Word of God.

When you exercise, you demand more energy from your body. The heart beats faster and more blood flow brings more oxygen to body cells, and your body responds to your demands in a natural manner. But *you* must make the demand on it *before* it will respond. Even your dog or your cat will respond to the command of your voice. *How much more shall your body respond to the demands made upon it by the Word of God spoken out of your mouth.* The truth is, your body always responds to your words in some manner, either for better or worse. So choose your words carefully.

Several years ago an article appeared in the Shreveport, Louisiana, *TIMES*, written by a neurosurgeon. The title of the article was "Talk to Your Body to Rid Ills." He was using a method which he called mental exercise which involves literally telling your body what to do.

He offered examples such as a diabetic who instructs his pancreas to secrete insulin or a person with hypertension to say, several times a day, "my blood pressure is 120 over 80."

He said, "It makes no difference whether the patient knows where his pancreas is or what 120 over 80 means. The body knows."

There is more truth to Mark 11:23 than most people realize.   You can have what you say in faith, but most people are saying what they have.

God created man's body to live forever, but sin brought the curse of sickness and death. The human body has an inherent ability to heal itself, but because of improper chemical balance and improper functioning of certain organs, certain medicines and chemicals will aid the body in the healing process.   But God's Word is the original and most powerful medicine available today.

It was His Word that created the human body.   It is the original medicine sent for the specific purpose of healing.   (Ps. 107:20.)

Medical science is finding that the principle of Mark 11:23 really works even to bring health to our physical bodies.

The words of Jesus in Luke 17:6 ring clear:

> **If ye had faith as a grain of mustard seed, ye might say unto this sycamine tree, Be thou plucked up by the root, and be thou planted in the sea; and it should obey you.**

The *INTERLINEAR GREEK-ENGLISH NEW TESTAMENT** says, "it *would* obey you." Jesus is not really talking about literal trees here, but problems you face in life. Whether you are calling for your blood pressure to be 120 over 80 or confessing that your pancreas secretes the proper amount of insulin, there is always someone that wants to accuse you of lying, because they don't understand these principles of faith. So, it is not necessary to make your confessions before others — make them to yourself in your own prayer time as you fellowship with the Lord.

Remember — when you are sick, call yourself well, for you are calling for what you don't have. If you put this into practice and make it a way of life, then your body will respond to your faith demands that are based on the authority of God's Holy Word.

No, it won't happen just because you say it, but saying it is involved in causing it to happen. Saying it is the way you plant the

---

*George Ricker Berry (Grand Rapids: Baker Book House, 1897 by Hines & Noble), p. 210.

seed for what you need. The spoken Word of God imparts spirit life into your physical body (John 6:63), for His Word is incorruptible seed, and it produces after its kind.

I challenge you to set aside a time by yourself, daily, to fellowship with God. Make it a practice to meditate His Word by speaking it to your body. Do it two or three times a day. Then double up on your confessions in the area where you have the most problems. Pray the Word over your body. Declare it to be true until you are fully persuaded. Your body will respond to your voice; how much more will it respond to God's Word spoken in FAITH.

Books by
Charles Capps

End Time Events
Hope – A Partner to Faith
Seedtime and Harvest
God's Image of You
Success Motivation Through the Word
The Tongue – A Creative Force
Releasing the Ability of God Through Prayer
Changing the Seen and Shaping the Unseen
God's Creative Power® Will Work for You
How You Can Avoid Tragedy
Faith and Confession
Substance of Things
Kicking Over Sacred Cows
The Light of Life
The Messenger of Satan
When Jesus Prays Through You
Faith That Will Not Change
Your Spiritual Authority
Faith That Will Work for You

Books by
Charles Capps
and
Annette Capps

God's Creative Power® for Finances
God's Creative Power® Gift Collection
Angels

www.charlescapps.com
or call
1-877-396-9400

Charles Capps is a retired farmer, land developer and ordained minister who travels throughout the United States sharing the truth of God's Word. He has taught Bible seminars for twenty-four years sharing how Christians can apply the Word to the circumstances of life and live victoriously.

In the mid '90s the Lord gave Charles an assignment to teach end-time events and a revelation of the coming of the Lord.

Besides authoring several books, including the best selling *The Tongue, A Creative Force,* and the minibook *God's Creative Power®,* which has sold 4 million copies, Charles Capps Ministries has a national daily syndicated radio broadcast and weekly TV broadcast called "Concepts of Faith."

For a complete list of CDs, DVDs, and books by Charles Capps, or to receive his publication, *Concepts of Faith,* write:

Charles Capps Ministries
P. O. Box 69 • England, Arkansas 72046

www.charlescapps.com
1-877-396-9400